Journeys

Journeys

SILLY BILLY'S WALK
TO LONDON
by Leon Rosselson

They called him Silly Billy. His parents had both died when he was very young so he lived with his uncle and aunt in a small town called Nether Wallop. His aunt kept house while his uncle mended clocks and watches. Neither of them ever travelled outside Nether Wallop.

"Why should I travel?" his uncle used to say. "Everywhere's the same as everywhere else."

Silly Billy wasn't very happy living with his uncle and aunt. They weren't cruel to him but they had little time to spend with him and quickly lost patience when he behaved foolishly.

"You're a sore trial to us, Silly Billy," his aunt used to say. And it's true that he was forgetful and dreamy and given to doing silly things. Once he put salt instead of sugar in the sugar bowl. His aunt stirred three spoonfuls into her morning tea and took a large swig. You should have seen her face! With a shriek and a gulp, she rushed off to the bathroom.

Another time, he put the cat in the fridge instead of in the garden. And once when he was sent out to buy faggots for their tea and came back with maggots instead – well! You can imagine the scolding, the wagging of fingers, the shaking of heads.

And it wasn't just the silly things he did which upset his uncle and aunt. It was the silly questions he was always asking.

"Why do our legs end in feet? How high is the sky? Where do we go when we're dead? When can I ride on an elephant?"

And on and on until his uncle, exasperated, would give him a clip round the ear and his aunt would shake her head sadly and lament, "You're a sore trial to us, Silly Billy, you are indeed."

One morning, Billy asked his uncle, "Why is the street at the end of the town called London Road?"

His uncle smiled. At last here was a question he could answer. "Because it goes to London, of course."

"Why does it go to London?"

"Because it's called London Road."

"Why don't we go to London?"

His uncle snorted. "What do we want to go to London for? Everywhere's the same as everywhere else."

Billy thought about this for a long time. He'd never been anywhere outside Nether Wallop. Could it really be true that everywhere was the same as everywhere else? Surely London would be different. London, so he'd heard, had streets paved with gold.

The next morning, instead of going to school, he decided to walk to London to see for himself. So when he left the house, he turned left instead of right. At the end of the town, he followed London Road. He walked and walked. He ate the strawberry-jam sandwich he'd brought with him. He passed fields with horses and cows grazing in them. He passed farms. He passed cottages and houses. He passed shops and inns. He passed an orchard and took two ripe apples from the trees. On he walked. People looked at him curiously but no one stopped to question him.

The light was fading. He was growing tired. His legs were aching. His feet were sore.

"Surely I'll reach London soon," he said to himself.

But it was no good. He was too tired to carry on. He took off his shoes to be more comfortable and lay down in the grass at the side of the road. Then he sat up. Supposing when he woke up he'd forgotten which was the way to London? He might set off in the wrong direction. So, very carefully, he placed his shoes so that the toes pointed to London and the heels to Nether Wallop.

"Now I'll remember which way to go," he said to himself as he fell asleep.

A little later, a tramp passed by. He looked at the sleeping boy. He picked up the shoes and examined them. No, they were much too small for him. He put the shoes back. But he set them down the other way round so that the toes pointed towards Nether Wallop and the heels towards London.

Silly Billy slept through the night and only woke when the rays of the morning sun caressed his face. He sat up, yawned and stretched himself. He looked at his shoes and smiled.

"Lucky I put them down so that the toes point towards London," he said to himself. "Otherwise I'm sure I would have set off in completely the wrong direction."

He put on his shoes and started walking. He passed an orchard and took two ripe apples from the trees for his breakfast. He passed inns and shops. He passed houses and cottages. He passed farms. He passed fields with cows and horses grazing in them. Sometimes the places he passed seemed like places he'd seen before. But then, he thought to himself, if everywhere is the same as everywhere else, that's not surprising.

At the end of the day's walking, as the light began to fade, he came to a small town. The houses seemed strangely familiar. He walked on. Suddenly he stopped, open-mouthed. He rubbed his eyes. That church. It was exactly like the church in Nether Wallop. But it couldn't be the same church because he'd been walking for two days *away* from Nether Wallop.

A little further on, he stopped again. He couldn't believe his eyes. There, on the other side of the road, was a watchmender's shop exactly like the watchmender's shop belonging to his uncle. It even had the same name over the doorway: J. Arbottle, Watchmender.

"So my uncle was right," he said to himself. "Everywhere *is* the same as everywhere else."

A man who looked like someone he knew passed by.

"Excuse me, Sir", Billy said. "Could you tell me the name of this town?"

The man looked at him hard to see if he was joking. Then he laughed. "You ought to know," he said. "You live here."

"I don't live here," Billy contradicted. "I live in Nether Wallop."

"This is Nether Wallop," said the man and walked away muttering, "The boy's crazy."

Billy was thunderstruck. Not only did this town look the same as Nether Wallop, it even had the same name. Somewhere between his Nether Wallop and London was another Nether Wallop identical to the first one.

He crossed the road and went into the watchmender's shop. Behind the counter was a grey-haired man who was the spitting image of his uncle. He looked pale and worried. When he saw Billy, he jumped up and shouted, "Agatha! Agatha! He's back! Billy's back!"

In rushed a woman who in every respect resembled his aunt. She seemed to have been crying. She flung herself on him and squeezed him and kissed him and shook him.

"Silly Billy!" she burst out. "You naughty boy. Where have you been? We've been so worried about you."

And indeed, she'd been out of her mind with worry because, although Billy was a sore trial to her, he was still her poor dead sister's boy and she couldn't bear the thought of any harm coming to him.

Billy was puzzled. "Excuse me," he said. "I think you're making a mistake. You don't know me."

The worry crept back into his aunt's face. Had the boy lost his memory completely?

"Don't know you?" said his uncle. "We're your uncle and aunt. You're our Silly Billy. We'd know you anywhere."

"It's true you look like my uncle and aunt," said Silly Billy. "But..."

Then he tried to explain how he'd been walking from Nether Wallop to London and how he'd arrived at another town called Nether Wallop which was exactly like the first Nether Wallop.

"But I live in the other Nether Wallop with another uncle and aunt, and I'm on my way to London," he concluded.

His uncle looked at him and shook his head. "Poor boy," he said.

"There, there," said his aunt. "You come into the kitchen with me and I'll make you a nice hot cup of cocoa and a strawberry-jam sandwich."

Then Billy knew for sure that this uncle and aunt were not his real uncle and aunt, because his real uncle and aunt had never spoken to him so sympathetically or treated him so kindly.

He went into the kitchen and drank the hot cocoa and ate the strawberry-jam sandwich. His uncle joined them and tried, with his wife's help, to persuade Billy that they really were his uncle and aunt and that this Nether Wallop was where Billy belonged. They tried in vain.

"I'm just passing through," Billy said, "on my way to London."

His uncle scratched his head. "Look," he said. "We're expecting our nephew to return. He's called Billy, too, and he looks just like you. So why don't you stay here with us until he does come back? Then you can continue on your way to London."

"All right," said Billy.

So he stayed.

His uncle and aunt were more understanding and patient with him than they'd been before, even though he was still forgetful and did silly things. And they tried to answer his questions as best they could. So Billy was happy, much happier than he'd been before he started his walk to London.

When Billy left school, his uncle taught him how to mend clocks and watches. He became so good at it that he soon took over the shop. And he never tried to walk to London again. In fact, he never travelled anywhere outside Nether Wallop.

"Why travel?" he used to tell people. "Everywhere's the same as everywhere else. Believe me, I know."

FEARLESS FRED AND
THE GHOST TRAIN
by Jane Irons

"Did I ever tell you about the time I rescued a drowning man?" said Uncle Fred.

"Yes, you did," muttered Tom through a mouthful of cornflakes. "Several times."

But Uncle Fred did not seem to hear. "I was only quite a young lad at the time," he went on, looking sternly at Jack who was spreading marmalade thickly on his toast. "About your age, but a good deal fitter than you are. I could swim, naturally. But there's a world of difference between doing a few lengths in a heated pool and plunging into a raging sea in the middle of winter."

"And that's what you did?" asked Sally, wide-eyed.

"Without a second thought."

"Oh, you are brave!" sighed Sally. "I could never ever do a thing like that." She sounded so sincere, anyone would have thought she really meant it.

"Nothing to it really," said Uncle Fred modestly. "Well, to give you the rest of the tale..."

However, at this point a violent outbreak of choking completely drowned his words.

"Sorry!" spluttered Tom. "Cornflake went down the wrong way."

"As I was saying..." said Uncle Fred.

"Uncle Fred," cried Jack, "I've just realized it's our last day! Do you remember you said something about a special treat?"

"Yes, yes," said Uncle Fred, rather annoyed by these constant interruptions. "I am perfectly well aware that it's your last day, and you don't have to remind me about the promised treat either. We are going to the fair."

The fair was a good idea, Tom and Jack were both agreed about that. But they were not so sure about going with Uncle Fred.

"He'll ruin it," said Tom, "like he ruins everything, by boring on and on. It's always the same old stories. 'How I cornered a dangerous criminal, how I captured a runaway tiger, how I saved an entire family from a blazing inferno.'"

"Well, we don't have to stay around and listen to him," said Jack. "We can go off on our own."

"Leave him with Sally, you mean?"

"Yeah, why not? She seems to actually like him, for some strange reason."

"Hmm," said Tom, not absolutely convinced. But then Sally was always so quiet and polite, you never quite knew what she was thinking. Perhaps she genuinely was impressed by Uncle Fred. Perhaps she was right, and Uncle Fred really was the fearless hero he made himself out to be.

I'll make a big effort, thought Tom. It is the last day, after all. I'll listen to his stories and I won't say anything. I might even try and sound impressed, too.

However, half an hour in the car with Uncle Fred was quite enough to put paid to Tom's good intentions.

It seemed that there was nothing Uncle Fred didn't know about fairs, and no ride – particularly the most daring and dangerous – that he hadn't tried when he was just a lad.

"So which rides are you planning to go on today?" asked Jack.

Uncle Fred hesitated a moment. "Well," he said, "I've got to be a bit careful now, you know, what with the arthritis in my knee. Still, I might just take a ride on the ghost train for old times' sake."

"I always find that a bit scary," said Sally.

"Oh, I'd never be scared by something like that," said Uncle Fred. "Just a bit of trickery, nothing more. Now your genuine ghost, that's quite another matter."

"You ever seen a ghost, then?" asked Tom, still trying to sound reasonably interested.

"Have I ever seen a ghost?" repeated Uncle Fred with slight scorn. "Why, the house I grew up in was positively infested with them. Used to bump into them all over the place. Lurking behind doors, gliding along corridors, walking through walls."

"And you weren't frightened at all?" queried Sally. "Not even one little bit?"

"Never used to bat an eyelid," said Uncle Fred with a careless laugh. "Takes more than that to frighten a fellow like me. Fearless Fred, that's what they used to call me."

At this point Tom gave an exasperated sigh.

"Cool it!" whispered Jack. "We'll lose him, double quick, just as soon as we get to the fair."

It was easy enough, in fact, to lose Uncle Fred. He was so busy explaining to Sally the internal mechanism of the Big Dipper that he did not notice the two boys slipping away into the crowd.

The next hour or so seemed to pass very quickly for Jack and Tom. They had two rides on the dodgems, one on the Jiggler, one on the Whirling Demon and one go each at the shooting gallery. At the hoop-la stall Jack won a green plastic frog – which they both agreed should go to Sally. It was at this point they realized they were down to their last fifty pence.

"We haven't even been on the ghost train yet," said Jack.

"Come on, then," said Tom. "If we meet up with Fearless Fred, he might just offer us a ride."

The ghost train was housed in a large tent, gaily painted with pictures of hollow-eyed ghosts, grisly skeletons, cobwebs as big as curtains, man-eating spiders and giant-sized bats.

Outside the tent a burly man was haranguing passers-by. "Want to be scared out of your wits?" he bawled. "Want a nice dose of the creepy-crawlies, the heeby-jeebies, the shivery-shakes? Want to jump right out of your skin? Then just step this way, ladies and gents, boys and girls, mums and dads, and take a trip on the Train of Terror, a trip you'll never forget."

"Of course," said a familiar voice, "it's all trickery. Nobody could really be scared by a tinpot outfit like that."

"Excuse me, mate" said the burly man to Uncle Fred. "I don't suppose you was referring by any chance to my world-famous, hair-raising, spine-chilling ghost train?" His voice was not friendly.

"Ahem," said Uncle Fred rather nervously. "Er, not exactly."

"Because if you was, mate," the burly man went on, starting to hustle Uncle Fred and Sally towards one of the empty cars, "I suggest you take a little trip, just so you knows what you're talking about."

"Hey, they're getting on," cried Jack. "Let's take the car behind. Wait for us, Uncle Fred, we're coming too."

There was no doubt about it: the ghost train was, as Jack remarked to Tom, "a total con job."

Admittedly, right at the start, before their eyes grew accustomed to the darkness, it was just slightly scary. Jack almost screamed when strands of something sticky and clinging brushed his face. Tom didn't like it much when a figure with a fluorescent rib cage and rattling bony fingers made a grab at his hair. But when he saw that the skeleton was wearing trainers, and that the glowing, spectral ribs were painted on a black T-shirt, he felt a bit silly and vowed not to be taken in by anything else.

"I mean, who'd be scared by *that*?" he remarked, as a weird wailing started up in the background, accompanied by hideous groans and the sound of dragging chains.

"Or that?" echoed Jack, as an ancient bat made out of tatty grey material fluttered jerkily to and fro on a wire above their heads.

So when a distant muffled cry – different from the other sounds – was heard, neither of the boys paid any attention. But they *were* surprised when the burly man suddenly leapt on their car and demanded money for the ride.

"We're with Uncle Fred – I mean the man in the car ahead," Tom explained. "He's paying for us."

"Ain't no one in the car ahead," said the man.

"But we saw them get on," insisted Tom.

"Who are you trying to kid?" said the man. "Come on, lads, pay up. Fifty pence each."

"We've only got fifty pence between us."

"What do you think this is?" said the man angrily. "Some kind of flipping charity? I'm running a business here, you know. I've got a living to earn. OK, so I'll take your fifty pence. But don't try this on again, understand?"

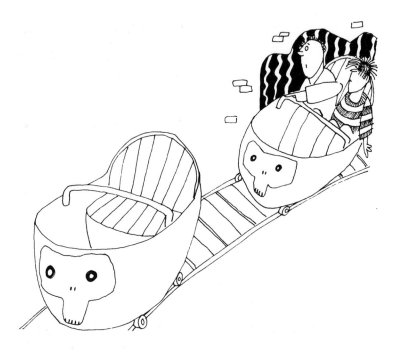

"What was he on about?" said Jack, when the man had gone.

"Don't know," said Tom. "Bit of a nutter, if you ask me."

Both boys, however, were quite relieved to see a glimmer of light round the next corner, and a moment later their car was rattling out through the swing doors into the bright sunshine.

"Hey!" said Jack. "That guy was right. There isn't anyone in the car in front! Whatever's happened to Sally and Uncle Fred?"

Sally hadn't cared much for the ride, right from the start. "Ooh!" she cried, as the car plunged into the blackness. "It's awfully dark!"

Uncle Fred, still huffing and puffing with indignation, made no reply. At the same moment, the air was suddenly filled with ghostly laughter mocking them from every corner.

"What's that?" said Sally in alarm.

"Oh, just some jiggery-pokery with a loudspeaker," muttered Uncle Fred, though he did not sound entirely convinced.

"Ugh!" exclaimed Sally, as something soft and furry swung across her face. "I don't like this at all. Can't we go back?"

"Don't make such a fuss!"

"It's crawling all over me!"

"Oh really!" exclaimed Uncle Fred crossly. "There's absolutely nothing to be afraid of. Another cheap trick, that's all." And, with that, he reached out and gave the strange furry thing a sudden yank.

The result, however, made them both jump. There was an angry screech and, in the same moment, a flash of light illuminated a dark creature with green eyes which seemed to be crouched menacingly just above their heads.

"What *is* it?" said Uncle Fred, and his voice now sounded less than steady.

"I think it's a cat," said Sally.

"No, no," cried Uncle Fred, his voice rising in panic. "It's not a cat, it's some frightful wild beast. Help!"

But his cry was answered only by a ghastly groan, as out of the darkness a fearful figure rose up beside their car, shrouded in luminous white.

"Who are you?" asked Uncle Fred in a quavering voice.

The figure, however, said nothing. It only laid a cold hand on Uncle Fred's throat.

"Aaargh!" cried Uncle Fred. "What do you want of me?"

"I am the ghost of the long-dead train driver come to claim my victim!" said the figure in a sepulchral voice.

"Mercy! Mercy!" cried Uncle Fred.

"It's only that man being silly," said Sally. But Uncle Fred was not listening; he was far too busy feeling frenziedly in his pockets and pressing money into the ghost's out-stretched hands.

"Take it!" cried Uncle Fred. "Take it all, only leave me in peace!"

"Thanks, mate," said the ghost, stuffing the cash briskly into his luminous robes and melting speedily back into the darkness.

"What I can't work out," said Sally, more to herself than to Uncle Fred, "is where the boys have got to. I mean, they should be just behind us, but they're not. It's a stupid ride, anyhow, and I'll be glad when it stops."

The end, however, came sooner than Sally was expecting. For, all of a sudden, their car put on a wild spurt, lurched blindly round a corner and jumped right off the rails. The next moment they came to an abrupt halt in utter darkness inside what seemed to be a narrow tunnel, which was curiously lined with soft swaying shapes that swished and rustled together eerily.

"Where are we?" cried Uncle Fred, his voice half muffled by the strange shapes. "What are these awful things?"

"They feel like coats," said Sally.

"Ghosts, did you say?" cried Uncle Fred. "Yes, they are ghosts! Crowding all around me, whispering to me, tormenting me! Help! We're trapped in this frightful place forever!"

"No, we're not," said Sally, pushing back the coats. "We're just at the back of the tent. It looks like some sort of store room. Come on, Uncle Fred, I can see a way out."

The burly man was nowhere to be seen, but hovering near the entrance were two rather anxious-looking boys.

"Hey, where did you get to?" cried Tom. "We were really worried about you, Sal."

"Oh, I'm all right," said Sally, calmly.

"What about you, Uncle Fred?" asked Jack. "What happened? You look a bit pale."

"Me, pale?" said Uncle Fred. "No, no, trick of the light. Still the same old Fearless Fred. Ahem." A slight pause, and then he went on, "Did I ever tell you about the time that..."

But nobody seemed to be listening any more. In fact, it was Sally's tale that the boys really wanted to hear.

A GHOST
FROM THE FUTURE
by Wendy Douthwaite

"It'll be perfect, Gem," Mum had said enthusiastically. "It's such a wonderful place. I'll be able to finish my book; and Gran says she'll come down for August. Won't that be great?"

However, Gemma was not so sure. This long holiday had been Gran's idea, really. It was Gran who had told Mum about Horton Lodge being available to rent for the whole of the summer holidays. Mum, being Mum, had gone over the top with excitement. She had talked almost non-stop about the old house.

"Gran was born there, in 1922," she told Gemma, "and I used to go there when I was little, to visit my grandparents. The house was sold when Great-Grandmother Paulson died, the year that you were born. It's beautiful. You'll love it!"

Now, as she followed Mum and the suit-cases up the path, Gemma tried to feel enthusiastic. Fluffy yowled plaintively from the depths of the cat-box, which Gemma carried under one arm whilst struggling under the weight of her haversack on the other side.

"Never mind, Fluffy," Gemma soothed, stopping half way up the path to peer in at the ginger cat's frightened green eyes. "We're here, now." She hoped Fluffy would settle in. Cats don't like moving from their home, Gran had said. If you're not careful, they run away and you never see them again.

As Gemma looked up at the old house, Mum's words echoed in her head. Beautiful was not the word she would have used. It was a grey house, with granite-grey stone walls and a browny-grey roof. Once, the window-frames had been painted white and the door blue, but now the paint was peeling and the colour had faded. Dark green ivy crept across the walls, its tendrils like long green fingers tapping against the window panes. To add to the gloomy feel of the house, dark clouds glowered above it, and thunder rumbled and grumbled in the distance.

"Come on!" Mum had hurried up the path, and now she was beckoning from the door-way. "Come and see Gran's old home!"

As they explored the house, Gemma had to admit that Horton Lodge wasn't so bad inside. Up in the attic, Mum opened a door which led into a room with a low, sloping ceiling, and a window which looked out across the valley.

"This used to be Gran's room, when she was a little girl," Mum said. "I used to sleep here when I came to stay, years ago."

"It's sweet," Gemma said. "Can I sleep here?"

Gemma was used to being on her own. Dad had died nine years ago, and since then Mum had had to work hard. She was a writer, supplementing her income with supply-teaching, and Gemma often looked after herself. When Anna and Steve had been at home, they had looked after their little sister but, now that they were both at work, Gemma was often on her own. She didn't mind. As long as there were books around, she was happy. And there *were* books at Horton Lodge.

"Some of these have been here since Gran's time," Mum said. "They must have stayed here, in this bookcase, and passed from owner to owner."

That night, Gemma took one of the old books up with her to the room in the attic which had been Gran's. The book was about the area around Horton Lodge, earlier in the century. Things which had happened over half a century earlier came to life in Gemma's mind as she read of disasters and celebrations, and her eyes widened in horror as she read of a fatal train crash which had taken place just a few miles from Horton, in 1933.

Gemma fell asleep with the light still on, Fluffy asleep at her feet, and the book draped across her chest.

It was the next morning when Gemma saw the train. She had been exploring Gran's old bedroom, where she herself was sleeping now, and had opened a cupboard in one corner. It was a large cupboard, the kind you could stand up in, and it had a tiny slit window which lit the cobwebs hanging from the ceiling, and a stack of cardboard boxes. Gemma picked up one of the boxes and backed out into the daylight.

On the box, in faded ink, were the letters E.M.P. Gemma recognized them straight away as Gran's initials when she was young, before she was married. Eleanor Margaret Paulson. Gran must have left the box here, all those years ago. Carefully, Gemma lifted the lid. Inside, wrapped in tissue paper, was a faded yellow dress. It had a square neck and short sleeves, wide braiding around the neck and waist, and ribbon ties at the back. Gemma held it up against her. It was about her size. It must have been one of Gran's dresses, when she was Gemma's age.

Gemma rummaged through the box. There were black shoes, shiny, with straps and buttons, and white socks, yellowed with age. There were also some toys; a knitted duck with a hat and moth-holes; an old battered teddy with one eye; and – tucked into the pocket of the yellow dress – a blue-and-white glass marble. Gemma brought it out and fingered it, holding it up to the light to admire the colours, before returning it to its pocket.

Quickly, Gemma pulled off her jeans and T-shirt, dressed herself in the old clothes, and then went to look at herself in the mirror by the window.

She closed her fingers around the marble in the pocket of the dress, and it was then that she saw the train. It was chugging its way across the valley, with a long cloud of smoke above it.

Downstairs, in the back living room, Mum was in no mood to listen. "I'm just in the middle of a really vital bit," she told Gemma, her voice vague and far away. Gemma sighed. Why hadn't Mum mentioned a railway line which ran so close to the house? And surely there was something *wrong* about that train? Oh well, she would just have to find out for herself.

Down the front path Gemma ran, across the lane, over the gate and through the field; she ducked under the wire, and there she was, at the railway station. She stood, panting, and looked about her, wondering why Mum hadn't mentioned a railway station. They could have come on holiday by train, instead of that tiring journey in Mum's battered old car, which had nearly given out on the way to Horton Lodge.

"Mornin', Miss."

The man looking down at Gemma smiled in a friendly way from beneath a long, droopy moustache that made her want to laugh. He wore a navy, high-buttoned coat, navy trousers, and a navy cap. Somehow, his clothes looked uncomfortable... and *wrong.*

Puzzled, Gemma looked around her; and then she saw the old posters on the wall, and a slot machine with chocolate bars. "Oh, I see..." she said, slowly, returning the man's smile. "This is one of those *old* railway stations. Mum took me to one, once."

"Well..." the station master began, pushing his cap further back and scratching his head thoughtfully, "I suppose it *has* been around a fair while."

"And there are *steam* engines," Gemma persisted.

He peered at her oddly. "Of *course* there are steam engines," he replied.

Then Gemma saw Great-Grandmother Paulson. She recognized her from the photograph in Mum's bedroom at home. But Great-Grandmother Paulson was not in faded sepia, and surrounded by a black frame. She was real, and moving; talking and laughing with her daughter, Eleanor, who was sitting beside her on a wooden bench on the station platform. The big wide-brimmed hat, pulled down to the top of Great-Grandmother's eyes, which Gemma had gazed at many times in the photograph, was not just a dark blur. It was navy-blue, and Great-Grandmother's dress was pale blue, with navy-blue flowers; and her shoes were shiny blue, with buckles.

Gemma was staring. She knew it was rude to stare, but she couldn't help it. It wasn't every day that you found yourself gazing at your great-grandmother, who looked young and pretty, and your grandmother, who was about your own age!

At last, Eleanor noticed her. "Hello," she said, smiling. "I've got a dress just like yours at home!"

Sixty-two years back in time, and Gemma couldn't think what to say. "I – I –" she stammered.

Great-Grandmother Paulson stood up. "We can't stay," she warned her daughter, giving Gemma a quick smile. "Our train will be here in a few minutes."

"We're going to London," Eleanor explained to Gemma, her eyes shining with excitement. "I've never been to London. We're going to stay with my aunt."

Gemma's gaze strayed away from them for a moment, and settled on a man sitting on the next bench, reading the daily paper. Her eyes picked up the date, printed on the front page. July 15th, 1933. Gemma felt herself go pale, and at last she found her voice. "You can't!" she cried. "You *mustn't*!"

But Great-Grandmother Paulson was already leading her daughter by the hand, towards the Ladies' Waiting Room. Gemma started to run after them, but then she saw a boy of about her own age, sitting by the fence. His knees were pulled up under his chin and he was chewing on a piece of grass. "Can you help me?" she asked, breathlessly. "*Please*. It's really important."

The boy looked up, interest lighting his brown eyes. He had a round, sun-tanned face, and his hair was dark and untidy. "What is it?" he asked.

"It might work," the boy said, when Gemma had explained. "I'll do my best."

When Gemma had found her great-grandmother, she pulled her over towards a patch of rough ground behind the station. "He's there!" she cried. "My poor brother. *Please* help me. I think he's broken his leg. I'm so frightened, I don't know what to do." She tried to imagine a disaster – Fluffy run over by a car, or Mum falling down the stairs – and she managed to force out some tears, which ran down her cheeks convincingly.

The boy, lying on the ground, groaned and cried out. The train hissed and squealed as it came into the station, covering everyone with clouds of smoke and steam.

"Oh dear," Great-Grandmother looked from one to the other, her eyes full of concern. "I want to help, but... we'll miss our train!"

Her daughter pulled at her sleeve. "We must help, Mummy," she cried. "We can catch a train tomorrow."

***

"And that's how I saved their lives, Mum. They missed the train, and then the boy and I ran away."

"Mmm. Yes, dear." Mum was reading through her day's writing. She stopped and looked down at Gemma, who was sitting cross-legged on the floor. "I think, daughter dear," Mum said, smiling, "that you have too much imagination. It's my fault, I suppose, for leaving you on your own too much."

"But Mum –"

"Besides," Mum added, turning back to her writing, "how *could* you have saved them? They weren't killed in that train crash that you read about. Neither you nor I would be here today, if they had been."

"But, Mum," Gemma began again, "don't you *see*? They were real and I was a ghost – a ghost from the future!" But it was no good. Mum was busy crossing out and rewriting, and she wasn't listening. Oh well, perhaps Gran would talk about it, when she came.

Gemma wandered out into the garden. She kicked at a stone, disconsolately.

The sun was going down across the valley, where the sky was pink and glowing.

The apple tree at the bottom of the garden looked black, etched against the bright sky; Gemma stopped to admire it.

"Hello, again," said a voice from the next-door garden. "I think you dropped this today. Would you like it back?"

A boy looked over the wall at her, holding out the blue and white marble. His face was round and sun-tanned, his eyes were brown and his hair was dark and untidy.

JOURNEY TO GHANA
by Geraldine Kaye

Heathrow Airport was all hustle and bustle. Kofi thought he had never been in such a busy place or seen so many people queuing. Kofi was eleven years old and his father had invited him to Ghana for the summer holidays. He wanted to go, of course. It was a long time since he had seen his father. Now he kept his eyes on the flight monitor above his head, watching the numbers go up on the screen. Suddenly Kofi's heart jumped like a frog.

"That's me, that's my flight, Mum!" he said. He wanted to get the goodbyes over and go now. Usually Kofi called his mother *Mum* or sometimes *Clare*. Calling your mother by her first name was a cool thing to do, but somehow Clare never seemed to stick.

"We'd better find Dianne," Mum said moving towards the barrier. "She'll be looking after you during the flight. Remember, in Ghana young people are expected to be very polite and obedient to their elders."

"So you keep telling me," Kofi said. "I'm always polite and obedient, aren't I?"

"You could have fooled me!" Mum said, teasing. "Come on."

"Are you Kofi Armah?" enquired a pretty Ghanaian air hostess in a blue uniform. "I'm Dianne. I'll be looking after Kofi during the flight," she told Mum, taking Kofi's hand luggage. "We're boarding in a minute. I'll take you straight through." Kofi's heart jumped again.

"How will I know my father at the airport?" he said.

"Don't worry, he'll know you," Mum said. "I wrote and said you'd be wearing your new green blazer. And remember, if your father can't be there your Aunt Albertine will meet you. Goodbye, love." She kissed Kofi and turned away quickly, her eyes filled with tears. "See you in September then."

"Goodbye, Mum," Kofi mumbled.

It was all very well for Mum to say all that about his father and recognizing the green blazer, Kofi thought, but *she* didn't have to fly to a new country all alone. He followed Dianne through security and passport control and then into a covered walkway which stretched like a huge caterpillar right into the body of the plane.

"I've put you by the window. You have family in Ghana?" Dianne asked.

"My father," Kofi said. "Doctor Isaac Armah. He works at the big hospital in Accra."

"In Ghana we say a child's spirit comes from his father," Dianne said. "I think I've heard of Doctor Isaac Armah."

The other passengers were boarding now. Most of them seemed to be Ghanaian businessmen in light suits. Kofi fastened his seat belt and stared out of the window. He could just make out the people waving in the terminal building but he didn't think Mum was one of them. She worked with computers and had to hurry back to her job. Had anyone noticed she was crying? For a moment Kofi wished he was safely back in their flat in Shepherd's Bush.

"Would you like orange juice?" said Dianne, holding a tray towards him. "I've got apple juice if you prefer?"

"Orange is fine, thanks," said Kofi, smiling politely.

The engines whirred noisily into life and the plane began to move. It went faster along the runway, shuddering and juddering. Suddenly it left the ground and rose like a great bird into the blue July sky.

Kofi looked down. It was like a map below, all squares and colours. White hotels, red roofs, grey roads, green fields and the silver line of the river Thames.

Kofi had last seen his father when he was three. He could only remember a little bit about him. He remembered his father's hand on the buggy, his voice as he leant over the cot, the one room where all three of them had lived. Both his parents had been students then, his father Ghanaian, his mother English. There had been arguments. Mum did not want to live in Ghana. The door had slammed as his father left.

Would he like Ghana, Kofi wondered. What should he call his father? *Dad* wouldn't be right for someone he hardly knew. Was *Sir* polite?

Kofi's father worked at a hospital in Accra. He had married again. Once he sent a snapshot of his house, "4, Hill Close".

"Does my father have any more children?" Kofi had asked when the aeroplane ticket came.

"A girl called Ama," Mum said vaguely.

A sister he had never seen. Kofi was quite excited.

"Will my father be at the airport?"

"Of course he will," Mum had said. "Anyway, your aunt will be there, and you've got his address."

Now Kofi got the plastic wallet out of his new blazer pocket. It contained his father's address and some Ghanaian money. Fifteen hundred cedis was about equal to one pound. Kofi was starting a new school next term and had persuaded Mum to get the new green blazer in advance. It was "cool". His father would probably wear a white coat in the hospital, like the doctors on the television. But would he be wearing a white coat at the airport?

"What's your name, my boy?" asked the passenger beside him.

"Kofi Joseph Armah, Sir," said Kofi proudly. "My father is Doctor Isaac Armah. He works in a big hospital in Accra."

"Eh-eh, I know that name. Everybody knows everybody in Ghana. Your father is a fine-fine doctor. Firstborn son takes his grandfather's name, it's all family in Ghana. At the end of the century we are still saying, 'The lone tree is soon blown down but the tree in the forest survives the storm,' just as our grandfathers did. I expect we shall say it in the next century too," the man said going back to his newspaper.

Kofi wondered about his name. *Kofi* just meant he was born on a Friday. Should he change to being called Joseph at his new school in September? Would that be polite to his grandfather and his family? But what would Mum think? Kofi was half-English and he belonged to her family too. Why hadn't she wanted to live in Ghana?

It was dark outside now. The air hostesses brought dinner round on trays. There were little dishes of roast chicken and peas, and fruit salad.

"Thank you," said Kofi, very politely.

"It's time you settled down," Dianne said, when she returned to the collect trays, half an hour later. "Close your eyes and try to get some sleep."

Kofi didn't feel a bit like settling down but he closed his eyes obediently and fell asleep.

He awoke to brilliant sunshine. Looking out of the window, he saw blue sea and palm trees and a lot of bare red earth. The plane was coming in to land and it hit the runway with a jolt. As soon as the plane stopped, all of the passengers started moving around and collecting their hand luggage. Soon everyone was streaming down the gangway and across the white concrete to the airport building. It was still early morning but hot already, like walking into an oven, Kofi thought.

Inside there was a flurry of excitement. Men and women in brightly coloured clothes were calling greetings as the passengers waited for their luggage. Soon everyone seemed to be laughing and hugging. Kofi thought that he had never seen so much laughing and hugging.

"Can you see your father, Kofi?" Dianne said as he looked all round the airport lounge. "My friend is waiting for me."

"Sorry," said Kofi. "I can't see him yet."

But with so many people, his father must be there somewhere, surely? Kofi stood by his luggage and tried to look "cool", but nobody came and he began to feel worried. Had Mum been wrong about his father recognizing him? Passengers left with their families and the airport building grew quiet. All the taxis had gone.

"Kofi Armah?" A plump woman was coming towards him holding out her arms. "Your father sends me to fetch you. I am his sister, Albertine."

"All right now, Kofi?" Dianne said.

"Yes. Goodbye and thanks," said Kofi as politely as he could with Aunt Albertine hugging him tight.

"Welcome, Kofi, welcome," said his aunt, over and over.

"Thank you, Aunt Albertine," Kofi said, out of breath from all the hugging. "I didn't even know my father had a sister until a few days ago."

"My beento brother has four sisters and his sisters have nine children," said Aunt Albertine with a thick-honey laugh which made him think of his father.

"What does 'beento' mean?" Kofi asked.

"A person who has been to England," said Aunt Albertine. "Isaac has gone to Karanda. I will take you to his village."

"But I thought he lived in Accra?" said Kofi.

"He does in the week," said Aunt Albertine, hailing a taxi which had just returned. "But the village paid for his education. He is their chief and he goes back there most weekends. Taxi-man!" she shouted as the taxi drew up. "How much to Karanda?"

"Forty thousand cedis?" the driver suggested. "Karanda is far-far."

"Eh-eh? What sort of a big price is that?" Aunt Albertine shouted. "Karanda is not far. You give me good price or I get another taxi."

The argument between his aunt and the driver took several minutes but finally a lower price was agreed. Kofi helped Aunt Albertine load her pile of new cloth into the taxi, as well as his own luggage.

"You are quiet, Kofi," Aunt Albertine said as they set off.

"I was thinking of my nine new cousins," Kofi said.

"Cousins?" said Aunt Albertine laughing. "The children of your father's sisters are called brothers and sisters in Ghana, so there is no quarrelling. And of course your father has children too, Ama and Ata and Bolo."

Three new brothers and sisters plus nine new cousins, called brothers and sisters, plus four new aunts! Kofi was too astonished to speak. What would he say to them? Suppose they didn't like him?

Kofi stared out of the window. At first he saw tall buildings on either side of the grey road with small houses built in between them. There were people in bright clothes everywhere, some selling melons or tomatoes, others selling hot roasted plantain or orange drinks, and all of them laughing and shouting.

Then the houses and people were left behind and the road was narrow and dusty red. Long-horned cattle grazed on either side and the boys looking after them waved as the taxi passed. Kofi waved back. Everyone was so friendly, he was going to like Ghana. But it was very hot. The sun was like a great yellow kettle boiling in the sky. Aunt Albertine had gone to sleep.

Eventually the road started to go uphill and the air was cooler. Tall trees with big green leaves shaded the road. Now and then they passed a group of huts, thatched with palm and bamboo. Mango and banana trees grew round each village, and there were vegetable plots too growing maize and sweet potatoes.

It was evening when they reached Karanda. Kofi just had time to see lots of huts with red-earth walls and corrugated-iron roofs. Was this where he belonged, he wondered. Then he was surrounded by children all jumping up and down and shouting, "Kofi, Kofi, Kofi has come!"

"Take him to his father," Aunt Albertine said and the children carried him along like a river. His father sat with the elders of the village under the shade tree.

"Greetings and welcome, Kofi, my first-born son," his father said, rising and holding out his arms. Instead of a white coat he was wearing a kente cloth, made of strips of gold and green and yellow silk sewn together. The kente cloth shone in the evening sun.

"Greetings to you, father," Kofi said shyly. He was glad he was wearing his new green blazer. "Greetings to the elders of Karanda, greetings to my family." Kofi knew what to say, his spirit came from his father. "The lone tree is soon blown down but the tree in the forest survives the storm."

"Eh-eh!" the elders said nodding and smiling. "This boy from England knows our Ghanaian ways already."

"Let us hear the song-maker's words to fit this day," his father said. The song-maker stood up and sang.

"Welcome to Joseph, son of our chief,
who has come from great England.
Welcome to Joseph, firstborn son,
he has come to Ghana land.
Awo, awo, awo."

When the song ended everybody clapped and clapped and then everybody was greeting Kofi and hugging him and laughing. Then the drumming started.

Kofi Joseph Armah had arrived in Ghana.

TO THE ADVENTURE
CENTRE
by Angela Bull

Faye was going to feed her rabbits, Roger
and Ringo, and Thumper, her Belgian hare,
but she stopped off on the way and peeped
into her brother Thomas's bedroom. Mum
was there, packing things into a rucksack.
Thomas was nowhere to be seen.

"Mum," said Faye, "does Thomas *have* to go on this adventure holiday?"

"Yes," said Mum, and she went on calmly packing.

"He doesn't want to."

"It'll be good for him," answered Mum.

"Why?"

"He should get outside more. He spends far too much time indoors with his computer games. Besides, the holiday'll be fun. Look at the brochure."

Faye turned its shiny pages. She saw life-jacketed kids crewing sailing dinghies; helmeted kids swarming up trees on ropes; kids swimming; kids with bows and arrows. None of them looked a bit like her brother.

"Thomas won't like it," she warned.

"He can give it a try," said Mum, fastening the rucksack in a final sort of way.

Faye went on searching for Thomas. She found him in the living room, flicking through a motor magazine, and frowning.

"I want to find a way of putting Dad's car out of action," he explained crossly. "Then I can't go to this horrible Adventure Centre."

"You couldn't possibly," said Faye. "You don't understand car engines."

"I've got to do *something*, and I don't know what else." Thomas sighed heavily. "If they just left me alone, I bet I could finish *Wizard's Quest* by tonight. I know how the spells work. Don't you wish there was magic in real life, as well as in computer games? Then I could use a bit to muck up the journey to the Centre!"

"There are ways of making journeys unlucky," said Faye, interested. "I read about them once, in a book at school. You have to meet a cross-eyed woman, or a hare, or a fox. Or you could break a mirror before you set off, or spill the salt."

"All the mirrors are screwed to the walls, and Mum won't let us have salt," Thomas grumbled. "So that's no use."

"So – " prompted Faye.

"So that leaves foxes and hares, or cross-eyed women, and we won't find any of those around here," said Thomas.

"Oh well, if you think so," said Faye, and she set off down the garden towards the hutches. It was annoying how people forgot that not all furry brown animals with long ears and fluffy tails were rabbits. There was Thumper, for instance… Maybe, if things went as she hoped, Thomas would notice the difference.

Soon after that, Dad arrived home to collect Thomas, and there was no time to meddle with the car engine, even if Thomas had known how. His rucksack, wellies, and sleeping bag were bundled into the boot, and Mum gave him a last hug.

"I haven't got my Gameboy – "

"You won't need it at the Adventure Centre," said Dad. "Off we go. Blast!" He swung the wheel violently, barely missing the gatepost. "Why doesn't Faye keep those rabbits under control?"

"Which one was it?" asked Thomas, as a white tail scuttled into a bush.

"The big reddish-brown one. Is it Thumper?" said Dad.

"Probably."

If Thomas hadn't been so gloomy, he might have been pleased to see Thumper. But instead, he just slumped in his seat.

"Well, no harm done," said Dad, "and we must get a move on. It looks as though there could be a thunderstorm."

Thomas glanced up at the sky. Blown on a sharp wind, black clouds had suddenly bubbled up from nowhere. They loomed heavily above. Soon raindrops were pattering down, harder and harder, and louder and louder. Waves of water blurred the glass. Dad set the wipers at their fastest speed. They whizzed to and fro, swooping, slashing; and the wind caught one of them sideways, and snapped it like a broken twig.

Furious, Dad pulled off the road. He leaped out into the downpour, and fiddled with the wiper. Thomas crossed his fingers for luck.

Dad scrambled back inside, a shower of drops falling from his clothes.

"Had we better go home?" Thomas asked hopefully.

"No need," said Dad. "There's a garage not far ahead. They'll soon mend the wiper for us."

Thomas's heart sank again. The car crawled forward, with Dad frowning through the streaming windscreen, and soon, much too soon, the garage lights beamed out.

"No; not a big job," said the garage mechanic cheerfully. He had the wiper mended in two minutes. "That should be OK. But take care. There may be flooding a bit further on. It's a bad spot."

"Dad," said Thomas, "if there's likely to be flooding, don't you think we should turn round?"

"If you're bothered about a bit of water on the road, how will you manage when you're crewing one of those super yachts?"

"I dunno," groaned Thomas.

The rain went on lashing down, trees tossed in the wind, and Thomas remembered vividly how sick he'd been when they'd crossed the sea to France last year.

Dad peered between the swinging wipers. "It's amazing how much water's gathered in this short time," he exclaimed. "Wow! Watch out!"

He stamped on the brake as the car hit a puddle the size of a lake. Grey fountains sprayed out from the wheels, cascading up, and crashing down on to the bonnet. The car lurched on to dry ground, shuddered, and stopped.

"Now we've soaked the spark plugs!" Dad groaned. "What an unlucky journey."

"Shall we turn round?" suggested Thomas.

"And drive through that flood again? Not likely. Besides, the car won't move. I'll try the houses over there, and see if anyone'll lend us a can of that waterproofing stuff to get us going again. You wait here."

Dad's hurrying shape was swallowed up instantly in the gloom. As he huddled alone in the car, Thomas's mind went back to the Adventure Centre. He imagined how icy drops would trickle over his helmet and down his neck as he tried – and probably failed – to climb ropes idiotically strung between trees. In weather like this you needed a computer, a few games for it, and a comfortable chair. Nothing else. Ropes and boats were for nutcases.

Dad, returning, directed a spraycan somewhere inside the bonnet. Then, he squelched back into the car, and turned the key in the ignition.

"Don't you dare start!" Thomas commanded silently.

The car took no notice. Slowly, grindingly, the engine coughed into life, and away they sploshed down the road, on towards ropes and dinghies. Taking a hand off the wheel, Dad wrung water from his hair, and wiped his dripping face on his sleeve.

"Hadn't we better go home before you catch a cold?" tried Thomas.

"I won't be beaten by a thunderstorm," Dad answered. "We'll reach your Adventure Centre somehow. But I don't mind if we stop for a cup of tea quite soon. I need warming up."

Any stop meant a few minutes less for outdoor fun, Thomas reflected, making the most of it. When they reached a café he spent as long as he could choosing a toasted teacake, a milkshake, and even a portion of chips to spin things out even more. There was a nice long wait for the food, as the café was crowded with other sheltering travellers. Outside the fuggy windows, the rain still poured down. The cars in the carpark were quite invisible.

"Honestly, Dad," said Thomas, dunking chips carefully, one by one, into his ketchup. "I can't see any point in going to an Adventure Centre if the weather's like this. I shan't be able to sail, or climb trees, or anything. It'll be a total waste of your money."

"We're not turning back now," Dad told him.

"You look frozen," Thomas said.

"I'll survive," said Dad, pouring another cup of tea.

Thomas dipped his chips in the ketchup, slowly and thoughtfully.

"I wonder if Faye broke a mirror?" he said.

"What are you on about now?" Dad enquired.

"It's one of the ways you can make a journey unlucky. You could spill salt or meet a fox," said Thomas, forgetting about cross-eyed women – and especially hares. "Faye read all about it at school."

"I should have thought she'd have better things to do," Dad retorted, rather snappishly. "Hurry up with those chips. We must get on."

They plunged out again into the dark and wet, stepping as best they could between the puddles. I wish Faye *had* broken a mirror, thought Thomas drearily, feeling the wind like a cold rope on his hands. He had completely forgotten how they had met Thumper by the gate.

"I don't believe it," Dad exploded.

Thomas stared through the gloom. The car stood where they had left it. Its buckled boot lid was flapping, half open, in the wind.

"A break-in?" he gasped.

"Too right," growled Dad. He lifted the lid, and eyed the empty boot. "All your stuff has gone! And we were only having a cup of tea."

"It's lucky I didn't bring my Gameboy!" exclaimed Thomas thankfully.

"I'll need to call the police," said Dad, "and a garage. And then we'll ring Mum."

"What for?" Thomas asked.

"Use your brain. You can't go to the Adventure Centre if all your gear's been pinched. You've got your wish. I'll have to take you home."

"Oh no," said Faye. "I didn't have any mirrors, or salt. But there were other things."

"I don't think we met a cross-eyed woman, or a fox," said Thomas. "I don't see how it could have been magic. It was just a thunderstorm that saved me from the Adventure Centre."

"Didn't you notice where I went, before you set off?" asked Faye. "It was down to the hutches."

"M'm?" Thomas murmured, not very interested. "Sorry, I want to finish *Wizard's Quest* just now."

Faye went into the kitchen, and collected some carrots. She carried them down the garden to her pets.

"Thank you, Thumper," she said. "You did very well this morning – even if Thomas hasn't said thank you."

Thumper looked at her, with big, wise eyes in his reddish-brown face. Then he sank his teeth into a carrot.

Faye was very proud of her Belgian hare.